# THE IMMORTAL John Lennon

1940 - 1980

# THE IMMORTAL John Lennon

1940-1980

MICHAEL HEATLEY

WHSMITH
EXCLUSIVE
· BOOKS ·

This edition produced exclusively for W H Smith

Published by
Octopus International
a division of Reed International Books Limited,
Michelin House, 81 Fulham Road, London SW3 6RB



ISBN 0-600-57635-3

Printed in Singapore

# Contents

# Liverpool to Hamburg

WITHOUT THE BEATLES, popular music as we know it today would almost certainly not exist. And without John Lennon, the Beatles would have lacked the driving force to change the face of the entertainment world and put the essential adjective into the Swinging Sixties.

The Beatles set blueprints that bands in the Nineties are still following with success. And though they had no single leader or lead singer, the compositions of Lennon and Paul McCartney were the springboard from which megastardom was attained. Aside from that, it was Lennon whose outspokenness caused headlines, Lennon whose peace campaigns in the Seventies made enemies of many who'd idolized him, and Lennon whose untimely death from an assassin's bullet in November 1980 stunned the world.

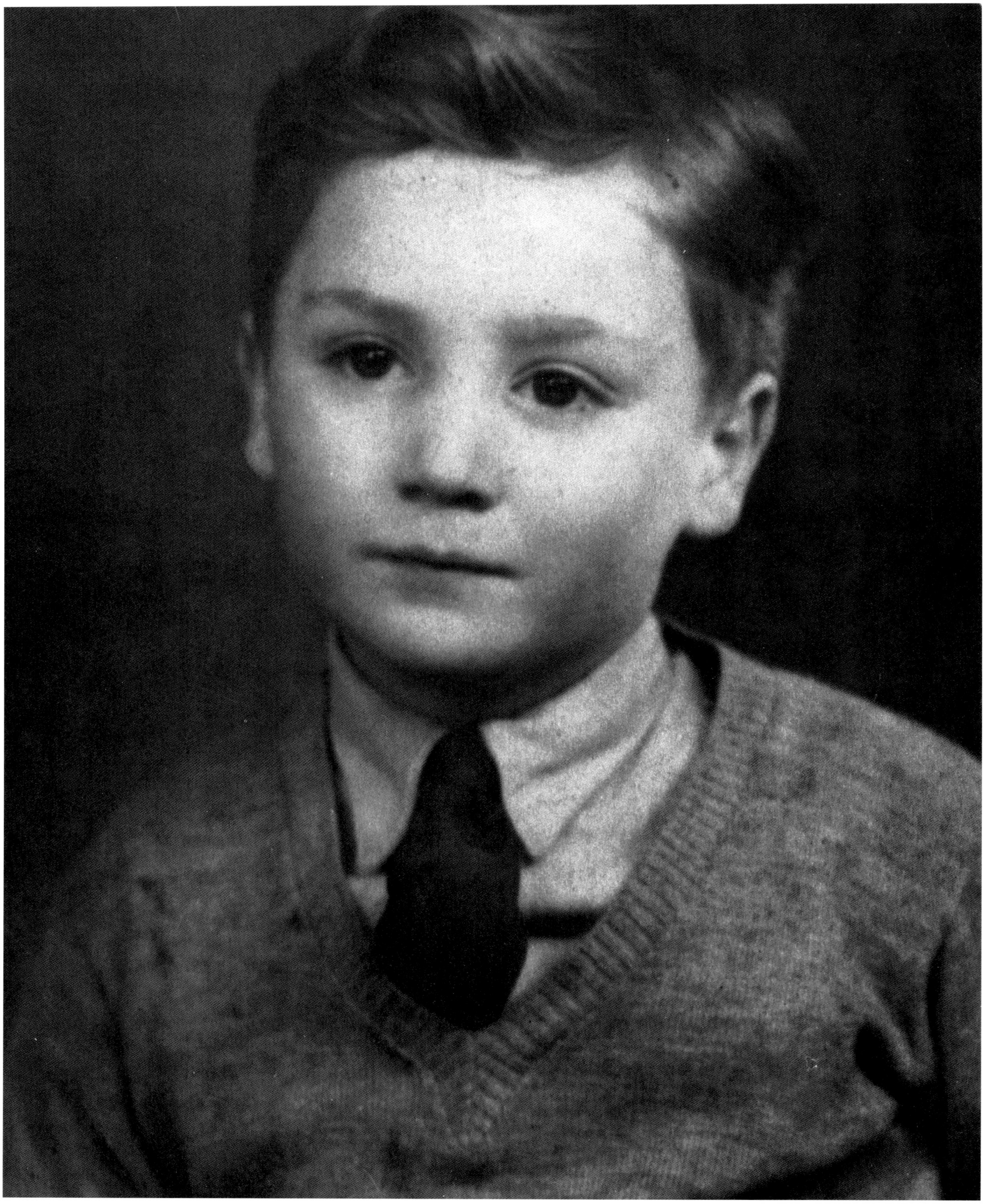

The mid-Fifties meeting of the young Lennon and a certain James Paul McCartney laid the foundations for the musical revolution to come. Some two years Lennon's junior, McCartney came from a musical background: his father (also named James) had been a professional jazz-band leader back in the 1920s. No one could then have guessed that James Junior, better known as Paul, would – with Lennon – be the mainstay of the most popular band the world had yet seen.

At first, McCartney wasn't impressed. 'His breath smelt,' he recalled later of Lennon 'but I showed him a few chords he didn't know.' The result was that he was invited to join the Quarrymen (*below*, McCartney and Lennon at the microphones), a skiffle group playing traditional American folksongs in the style of Leadbelly with acoustic guitars and a stand-up bass improvised with broom handle and tea-chest. Their name came from Quarrybank High School, where Lennon studied. He failed all his examinations, showing a lack of application that brought reports such as 'he is just wasting other pupils' time'. Despite this, John managed to get a place at art school in 1957, thanks mainly to a sympathetic headmaster.

The Quarrymen changed name and personnel almost monthly around the Lennon–McCartney nucleus. Rejecting the Moondogs and Rainbows for the Silver Beatles, they paid homage to Buddy Holly's Crickets, with a typical Lennon pun on 'beat'.

Lead guitarist was George Harrison, shy and retiring, yet far more able than Lennon and McCartney. Stuart Sutcliffe, Lennon's closest friend, played bass. When asked to join, Stu (*overleaf,* with George and John) admitted he couldn't play his instrument, but his dark, James Dean-ish good looks overcame any doubts. Drummer Pete Best (*left,* with Harrison, McCartney and Lennon), whose mother ran Liverpool's Casbah Club, completed the rhythm section when they journeyed to Germany to seek fame and fortune.

Far from Aunt Mimi's watchful eye, Hamburg was an exciting environment for the young John Lennon. Like Liverpool, it was a northern seaport whose streets teemed with the weird and the wonderful, and even though the lads were sleeping five to a room in the red-light district, the trip was an adventure of a young lifetime.

The patrons of the Indra Club, where Lennon played his first Hamburg engagement on 18 August 1960, wanted American music – black R&B as heard on US Forces radio. And they wanted lots of it – up to six hours at a stretch. With an average show back home just an hour in length, the fledgling Beatles soon found themselves writing songs to eke out those they already knew, and John and Paul took the lead. It was a learning experience that would stand them in good stead.

They eventually graduated to the larger Kaiserkeller, but their five-month residency effectively ended just before Christmas 1960 when George was deported: at 17 he was under-age to be in a club. Paul and Pete Best followed him home after they accidentally started a fire. They played Hamburg five times in total, but Stu Sutcliffe chose to stay on to pursue a painting career after the second stint. His subsequent tragic death from a brain haemorrhage closed a chapter, but in musical terms, this was only the beginning for the Beatles. With Paul switching to bass guitar, the line-up that shaped a generation of pop music was born.

John Lennon's life had begun, with a series of bangs, on the night of 9 October 1940, but Liverpool survived many such air raids.

When Lennon's father, Freddie, deserted the family, his mother, Julia, was happy for her son to be brought up by his Aunt Mimi and Uncle George. Julia Lennon returned at intervals, bringing presents to re-establish the bond between mother and son and it was one of these, a second-hand £10 guitar, that was to change to course of John Lennon's life and music history. Aunt Mimi (*above,* with John) didn't approve. 'The guitar's all right, John,' she observed in a remark that was to become legendary, 'but you'll never make a living at it.'

Lennon was reconciled with his mother before her death in July 1958, which was 'the worst thing that ever happened to me,' he recalled later. Twelve years on, the song 'Mother' showed the pain still endured.

THE CAVERN
THIS IS WHERE IT ALL BEGAN!
THE Cavern
TO LET

Back on Merseyside, the battle-hardened Beatles (they dropped the 'Silver' now) sounded impressive alongside the pop fare of 1961. They found their first residency at the Cavern Club (*left and below*), a

dingy, down-at-heel jazz club in Mathew Street, where they played at lunchtimes. They graduated to evenings and soon became the house band.

Among the visitors to the Beatles' lunchtime sessions were Cynthia Powell (later Mrs John Lennon) and Brian Epstein, a 27-year old record shop owner, whose curiosity was aroused by a fan asking for 'My Bonnie', a single the group had cut in Hamburg with Lennon on lead. It was when Epstein caught them playing at the Cavern Club in November that things really began to happen. By mid-December, they'd signed to his NEMS Enterprises; they were to be the first of a stable that was to include Gerry and the Pacemakers, Billy J. Kramer and the Dakotas, Cilla Black and others.

With Epstein's help, an audition was secured with Decca Records, one of the major pop labels of the time. Driven down to London by roadie Neil Aspinall on New Year's Day 1962, the Beatles recorded fifteen songs at the Hampstead studios. But Decca boss Bill Rowe was not impressed, insisting that guitar groups were 'on the way out'. Undaunted, Epstein took the audition tape to EMI, whose Parlophone label producer, George Martin, saw their potential straight away. After an audition, however, he insisted Pete Best be replaced by a more proficient musician.

THE
BEATLES
ARE AT
THE CAVERN
ON
TUESDAY NIGHT
19TH FEBRUARY, 1963
BE EARLY!
TELL YOUR FRIENDS!

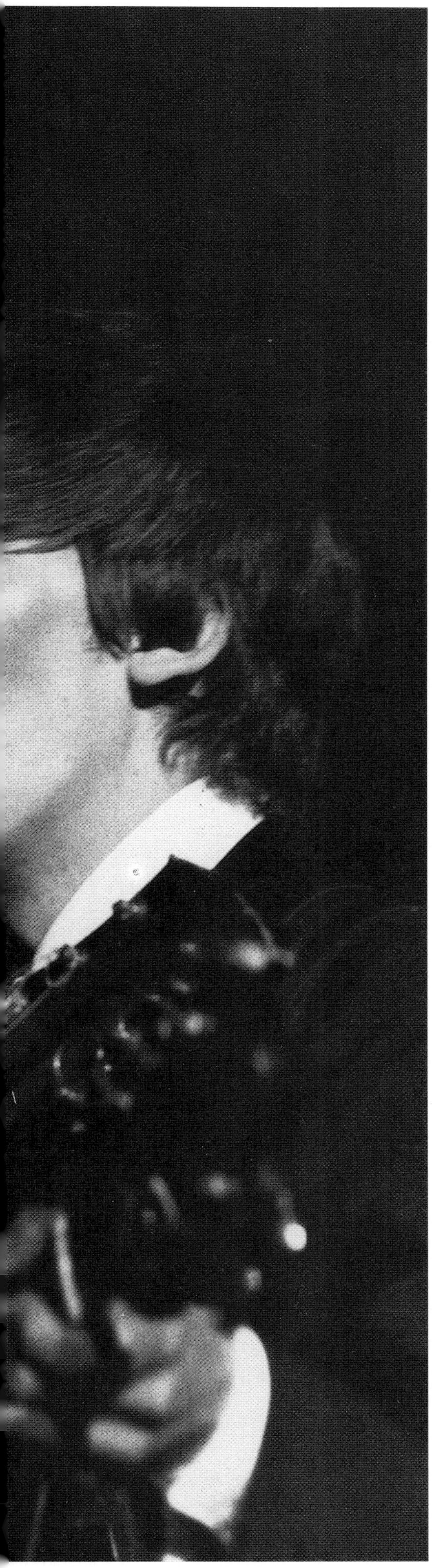

The Beatles' new drummer was Ringo Starr – real name Richard Starkey – from Rory Storme and the Hurricanes. He was another Hamburg veteran, but his accession to the drumstool in August was not greeted with delight by all Beatles fans. Something else that inspired mixed feelings was the news that Lennon's girlfriend, Cynthia Powell, was pregnant. They married on 23 August, a wedding reception being thrown by Epstein in a down-market Liverpool restaurant, where the couple were toasted in glasses of water. Son Julian, later a pop star in his own right, was born on 8 April 1963, though at the time few fans outside Liverpool realized Lennon was married, let alone a father.

In 1965 Lennon wrote to Cynthia expressing his feelings about fatherhood and fame. 'I spend hours in the dressing rooms…thinking about the times I've wasted not being with him [Julian]…I really want him to know and love me and miss me like I seem to be missing both of you so much.' Given a second chance with Yoko Ono in the Seventies, John then, understandably, chose to reject music in favour of fatherhood.

Ludwig
THE
BEATLES

# Beat and Beatlemania

FOR MANY PEOPLE, the Sixties began on 5 October 1962, the day 'Love Me Do' was released. John's biggest early influence had been Elvis Presley, but 'Love Me Do' was nearer Buddy Holly, with John's soulful harmonica thrown in. Public reaction secured the group a Number Seventeen hit and their first major appearance at Liverpool's Empire Theatre with Little Richard and others. It wasn't to be until May 1963, however, that they managed to top a package tour bill over Roy Orbison and Gerry and the Pacemakers.

Leaving the clubs was a wrench for Lennon. 'The music was dead before we even went on the theatre tour of Britain. We had to reduce an hour or two's playing to twenty minutes, and we would go on and repeat the same twenty minutes every night.'

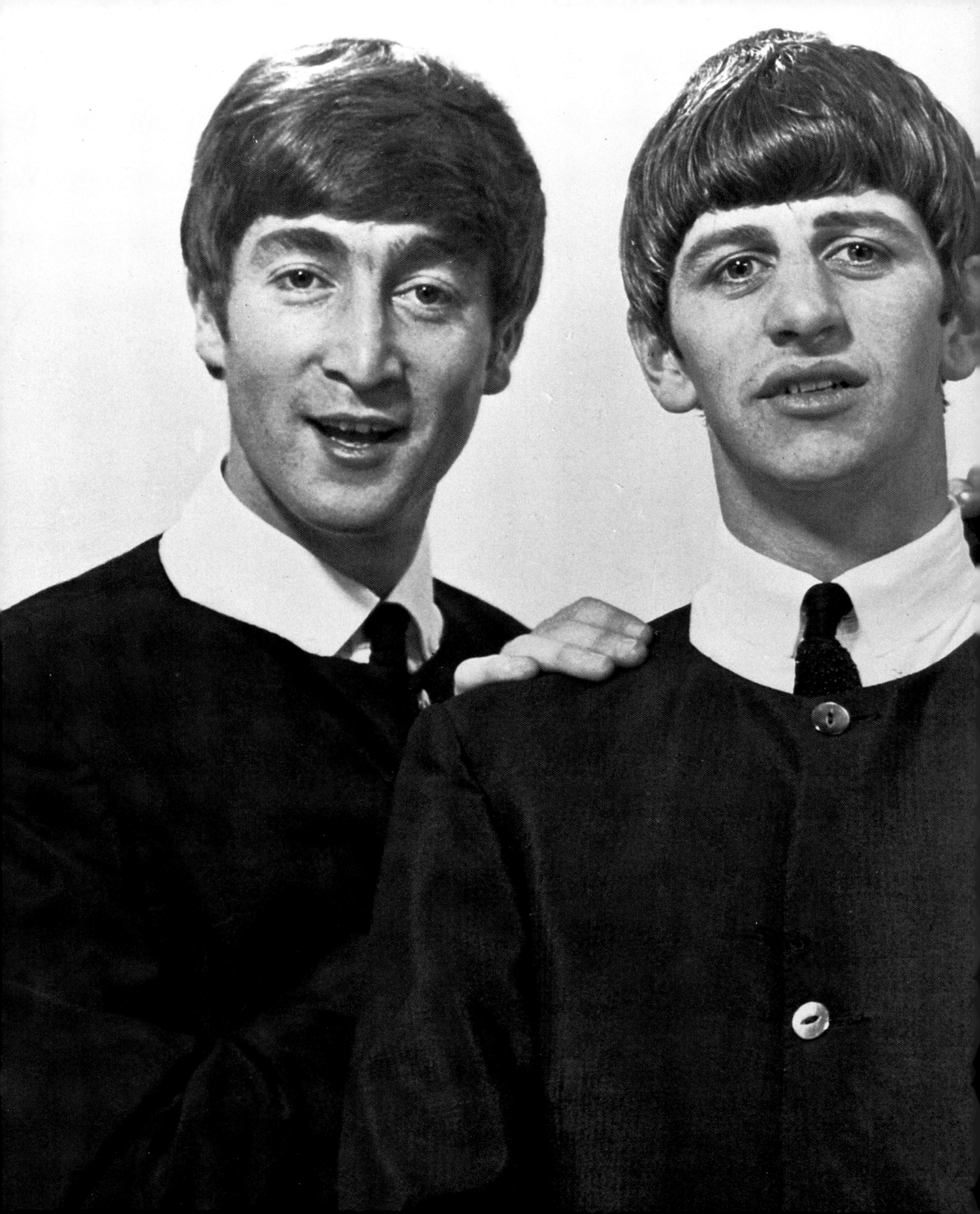

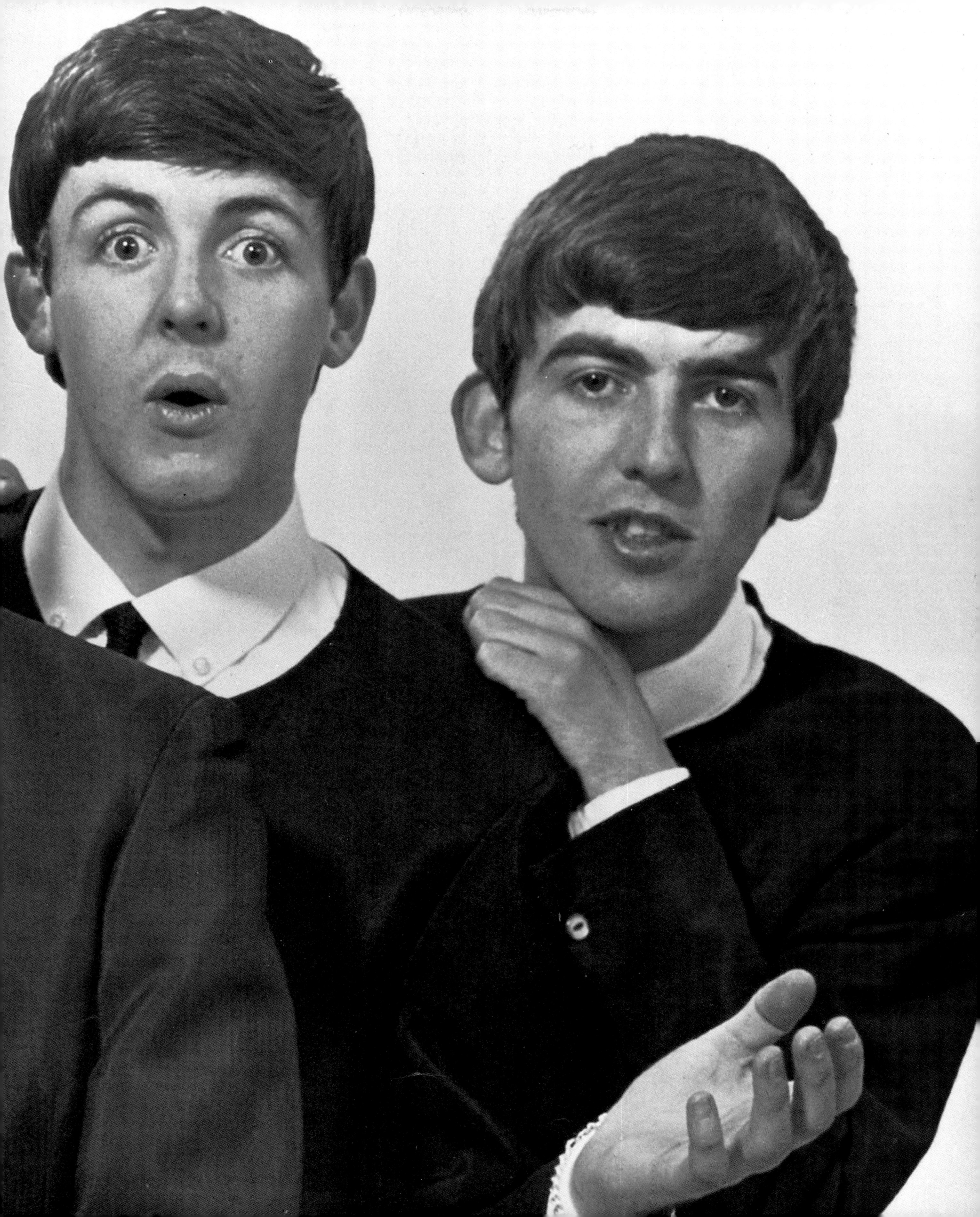

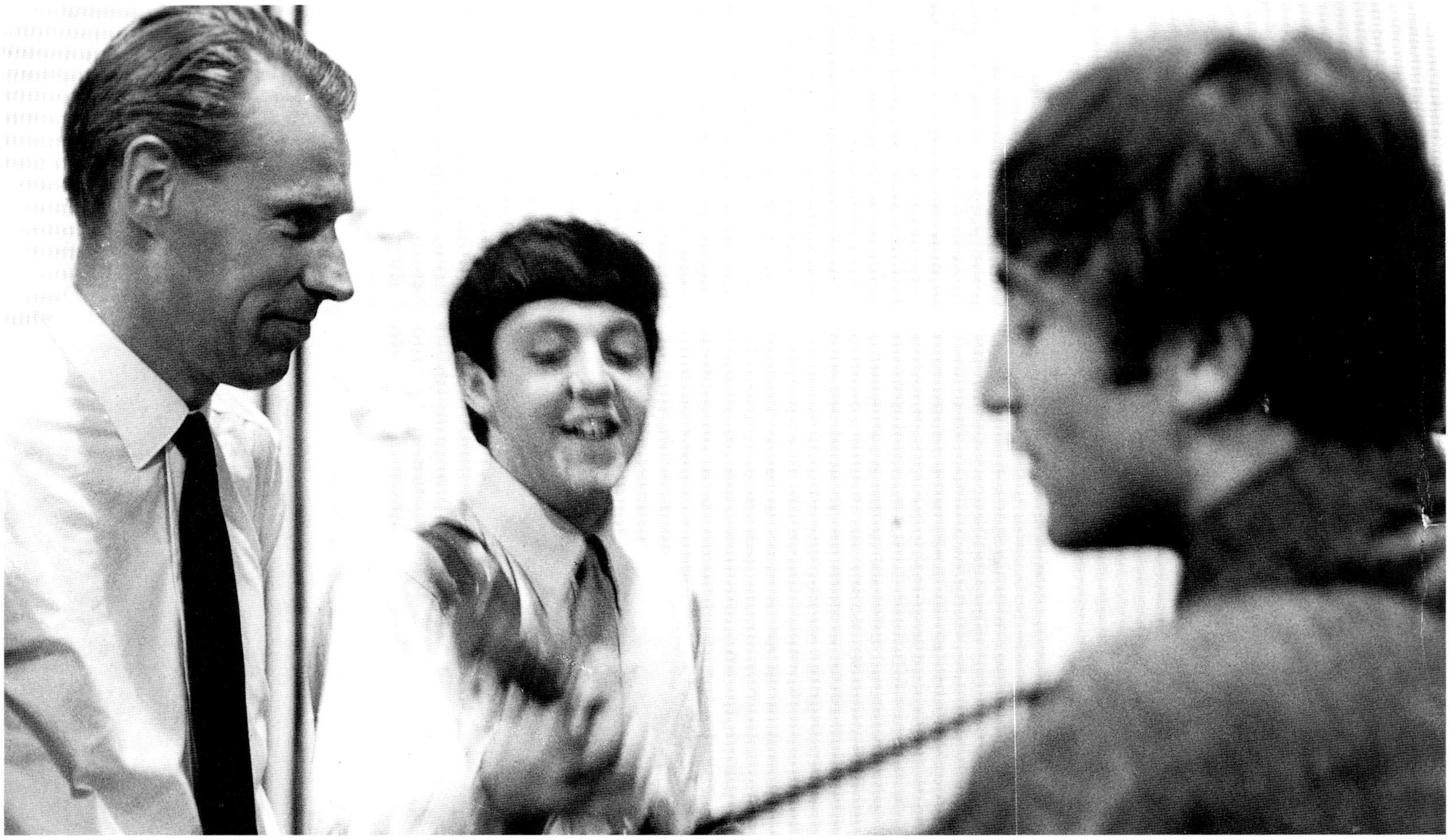

With George Martin (*above*) at the helm, the Beatles recorded their first album in April 1963. Completed in one marathon session, it was named *Please Please Me,* after their second hit single, and contained eight Lennon–McCartney songs alongside covers of material by Goffin and King, Bacharach and David and others. Though Lennon and McCartney wrote separately later on, these early efforts seem to have been genuine collaborations.

As their producer, Martin was in the ideal position to observe the two men at work. 'Paul needs an audience but John doesn't. John is very lazy: without Paul he would often give up. John writes for his own amusement.'

Their songs were initially simple affairs, many with 'love' or 'her' in the title and often clocking in at under two minutes. Their models were classic American pop of the Brill Building school and the black pop of the Miracles and the Shirelles, but Lennon's humour bubbled through, infusing McCartney's more straight-laced pop with a dash of typically Liverpudlian wit. It was obviously the ideal combination.

VOX

The term Beatlemania (first coined by the *Daily Mirror* newspaper) sprang into being as the reaction to the group's personal appearances. In the autumn of 1963 newspapers carried reports of hundreds of young people blocking the streets outside the London Palladium before a televised performance. In fact, according to veteran photographer Dezo Hoffman, no more than eight girls were waiting outside: newsmen expecting a riotous assembly simply invented one.

True or not, the reports inspired a reaction that needed no imagination. Returning from a short Swedish tour in October to a packed London

airport, the Beatles discovered that the nation's youth had taken their cue from the popular press and life was never to be the same again.

The group were a newspaper writer's dream: there were stories of boys being sent home from school for their 'Beatle' haircuts, while the Beatles themselves escaped from fans at Birmingham by disguising themselves as policemen. It was all good ammunition in the circulation war; one paper carried five front-page Beatles stories in a single week.

Fuelled by such tabloid fodder, Beatle fans could be obsessional in their devotion, often to one Beatle in particular. Later in the group's career, the Apple Scruffs, a group of specially devoted fans, would camp outside the group's offices and recording studios for a glimpse of their idols. In the early days, though, anything could happen: a chance remark by John and George that they liked jellybabies led to them being pelted with the sweets on stage. The Beatlemania years were, said Lennon, like 'living inside a goldfish bowl'.

As Beatlemania raged, live shows were becoming more and more of an irrelevance. With screaming crowds at every corner, there was no privacy, while the noise at live concerts made it arguable whether it made any difference if their guitar leads were plugged in or not.

'It happened bit by bit,' explained Lennon, 'gradually until this complete craziness is surrounding you…' Being trapped by teenage fans, however adoring, was no fun whatsoever, and playing was less than enjoyable if all the time you were wondering exactly how you were going to emerge from the theatre with your limbs and senses intact.

George and John were first to make their reluctance to play live known. Although the press were privy to backstage arguments, they rarely if ever printed them. The Beatles were a national institution and a source of newsworthy stories. Why rock the boat, they reasoned?

Lennon, for instance, was quick to rebel against the 'Moptop' image, the suits and the squeaky-clean look, Epstein had planned. 'Brian put us in neat suits and shirts, and Paul was right behind him. I didn't dig that, and I used to try to get George to rebel with me. My little rebellion was to have my tie loose, with the button of my shirt undone.'

Touring also meant glad-handing local dignitaries, something Lennon in particular couldn't stand. 'It was a complete oppression,' he recalled later. 'I mean, we had to go through humiliation upon humiliation, the middle classes and showbiz and Lord Mayors and all that. They were so condescending and stupid. Everybody trying to use us. It was a special humiliation for me,' he continued, 'because I could never keep my mouth shut and I'd always have to be drunk or pilled to counteract this pressure. It was really hell…'

Musically, he still felt the Beatles had it in them to be great, if only they had the chance. 'What we generated was fantastic: when we played straight rock there was nobody to touch us in Britain. As soon as we made it, the rough edges were knocked off.' And for the rawest and most rebellious of the Fab Four, that refining was to become increasingly hard to take.

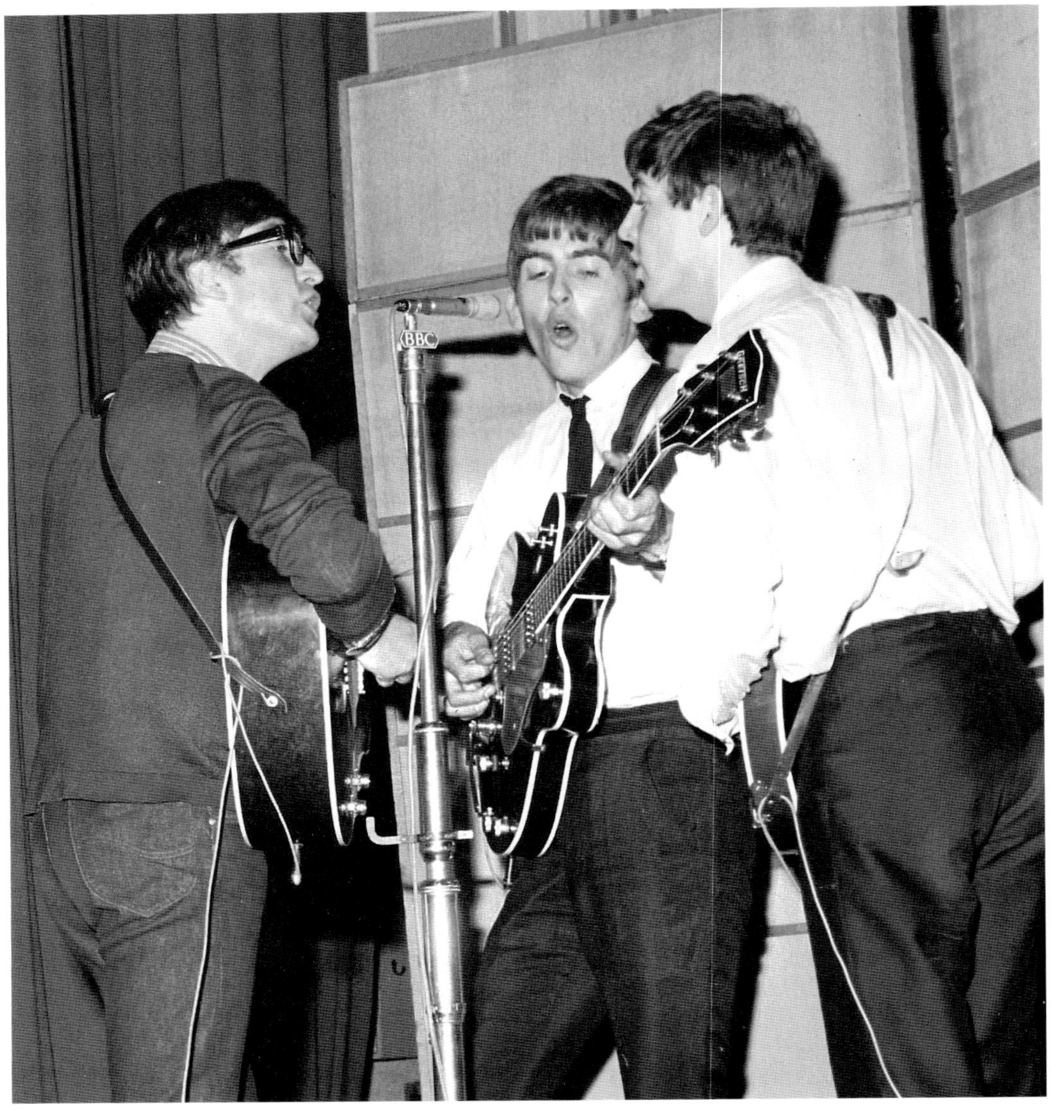

Away from the madness of live performance, the studio became a creative tool in the Beatles' hands. Aided by George Martin, they created ever more stunning music.

They were the first pop group to be accepted by the Establishment, yet Lennon's relationship with authority was strained at best. Sometimes he'd try to turn his unease into humour: at the Royal Command Performance he urged, 'Would the people in the cheap seats clap your hands – the rest of you rattle your jewellery...' At other times he was more serious: the MBE John received from the Queen with his fellow Moptops in October 1965 (*right*) was returned in 1969 in protest against the Nigerian civil war.

When his first book, *In His Own Write*, won the prestigious Foyle's Literary Prize in March 1964, John's entire acceptance speech was 'Thank you very much. You've got a lucky face!' He then fled.

PAN AMERICAN
N704PA
THE BEATLES
BRITISH EUROPEAN AIRWAYS
PAN AM
PAN AM

When the Beatles arrived in America for the first time in February 1964 (*left*), John was just 23 and clearly excited. 'Conquering America was the best thing,' he said of the period. 'We wanted to be

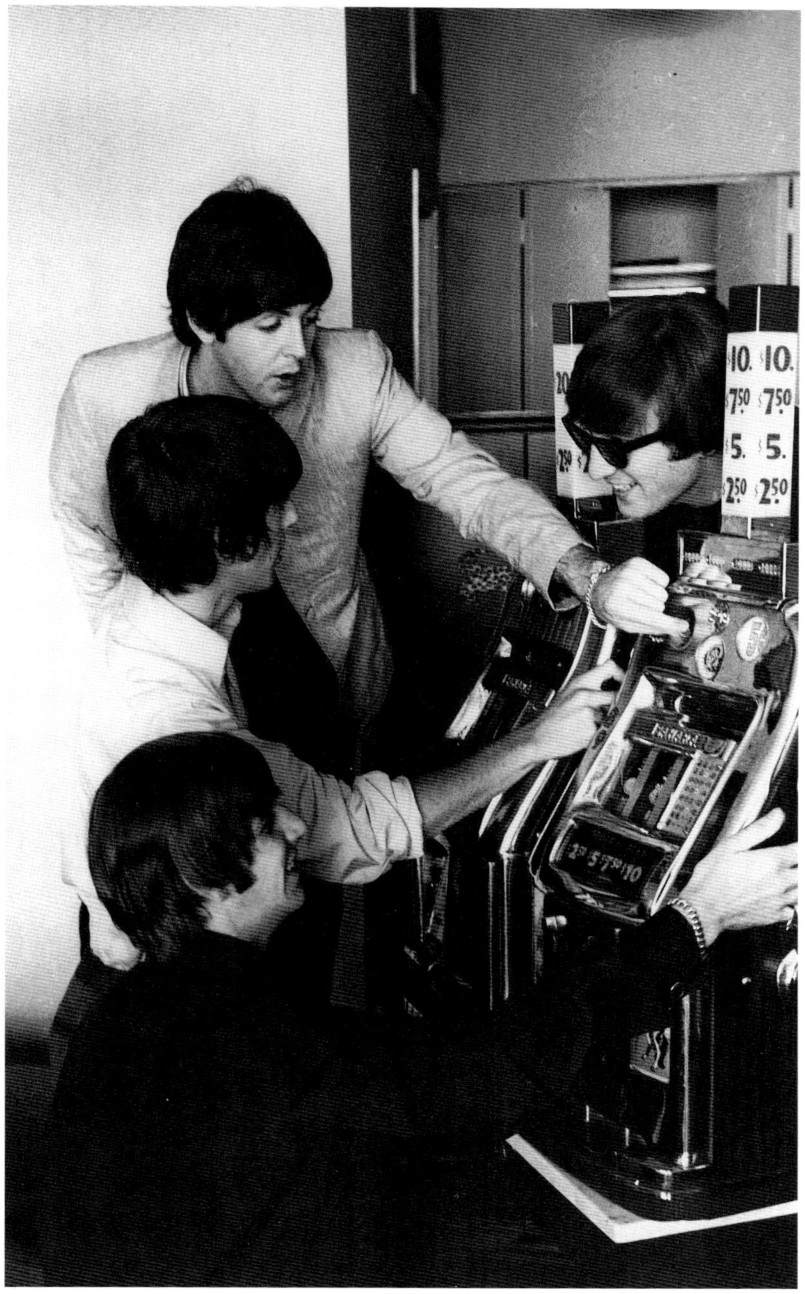

bigger than Elvis.' In 1964 they were. In April 'Can't Buy Me Love' topped the charts on both sides of the Atlantic, and it was now clear that Beatlemania ruled worldwide.

The Beatles' popularity had been slow to start in the States, and the situation hadn't been helped by a small label, VeeJay, being granted the rights to the first releases before Capitol Records (EMI's American arm) realized they'd signed away a goldmine and quickly changed their minds. Even allowing for this less than perfect beginning, the Beatles accounted for 60 per cent of all records sold in North America during February 1964 – a staggering statistic and one unlikely ever to be repeated.

The first American tour followed three weeks of successful dates in France. The day before they flew from London to New York, Paul commented: 'They've got everything over there. What do they want us for?' For John, it was the culmination of a dream that started with all-American performers like Elvis and Bill Haley. As a youth, he'd been to see *Rock Around The Clock,* and had been 'all set to tear up the seats [of the cinema] but nobody joined in'. As he was soon to find, America's reaction to the Beatles was to be rather more enthusiastic.

In the history of rock from Elvis onwards, the flow of music from the US to Britain had been all but unreciprocated. With the 1964 Number One success of 'I Want To Hold Your Hand', the one-way traffic suddenly changed direction. As earlier Beatles singles followed it up the chart, April 1964 saw the top five positions occupied by the group.

They'd been assisted by TV appearances on prestigious programmes like Ed Sullivan's nationally broadcast show (*right*), on which they gave their first live US TV performance in February 1964. Disc jockey Murray the K, the self-styled 'fifth Beatle', was another influential figure to get behind the group early on.

The year ended with 'I Feel Fine' atop the *Billboard* charts. Incredibly, it was the group's sixth American Number One single of the year.

Their third American tour included just sixteen concerts – but one was August 1965's gig at New York's Shea Stadium, at which the Beatles entertained a world record 56,000 fans and earned an equally staggering $160,000. It wasn't always laughter all the way to the bank, however. A casual remark that the Beatles were more popular than Jesus Christ on the eve of an American tour put Lennon in fear of his life and provoked Beatle-burning demonstrations with bonfires of Fab Four discs. In a Chicago press conference John apologized for giving offence while reserving the right to hold controversial opinions.

Released in 1966, the Beatles' seventh LP, *Revolver,* was their transitional album from the pure pop of the previous year's *Rubber Soul* to the full-blown psychedelia of 1967's *Sgt Pepper.* Songs like 'She Said She Said', written by John after taking the mind-expanding drug LSD, showed the change clearly. 'It was only the second trip we'd had,' revealed Lennon. Pills had been a part of life in Hamburg, but this was something different. 'Tomorrow Never Knows' was another surreal, psychedelic song, with the lyrics quite clearly owing a great deal to Timothy Leary and *The Tibetan Book of the Dead.*

Lennon's 'Strawberry Fields Forever', a double A-side with 'Penny Lane' in early 1967, was even more stunning, with its surreal, almost nonsensical, lyrics and had been originally intended for inclusion on *Sgt Pepper* later in the year. It was quite a step on from the pop songs of 1964's *Beatles For Sale.*

While Paul had been perfecting the act of the three-minute pop song (and, it must be said, succeeding brilliantly), John had been seeking ways of utilizing the literary talents shown in his books *In His Own Write* and *Spaniard In The Works. Revolver*'s more ambitious musical settings provided him with many more options.

He had also tried the folk-rock confessional format for size, lyrics emphasized by a sparse uncluttered backing *à la* Bob Dylan. The 1965 soundtrack to *Help!* showed that Lennon took aboard a large dose of Dylan to produce a song like 'You've Got To Hide Your Love Away'. *Rubber Soul*'s 'Norwegian Wood' was similar in its diverse lyrical content and simple, strummed acoustic guitar backing, and Lennon later explained he was writing about an affair without letting his wife in on the secret.

Songwriting had earlier been seen as a strictly commercial skill, as Paul McCartney was to recall. 'We used to say "let's write a house", then we'd say "let's write a car". Finally it was "let's write a swimming pool".' Those days were clearly over and, as their songwriting became much more of an exercise in self-fulfilment, by the mid-Sixties the Lennon–McCartney partnership had become one that existed in name only.

John's marriage had initially been concealed from the fans, but the news inevitably got out after the birth of Julian (*right*, with his father). Marriage had proved the death knell for pre-Beatles artists like Marty Wilde, whose fans had deserted him *en masse* for other, more eligible idols, but the Fab Four's success was based on far more than mere sex appeal. And in John's case it was the marriage that suffered, not the career. Cynthia (*above*) bore all the stresses and strains with uncomplaining good grace until she returned from a holiday in Greece to find she had been usurped by Yoko Ono. She sued for divorce in 1968.

The filming of *Help!* (*left*), the Beatles' second movie, co-starring Leo McKern and Eleanor Bron, gathered almost as large crowds as their concerts – whether in the Bahamas, Austria or England's windy Salisbury Plain. The end result also pulled large audiences on its 1965 release and was a triumph, inspiring critical comparisons with the Marx Brothers. The plot was suitably ridiculous, involving the gift of a ring to Ringo from a fan, and the group's globetrotting attempts to avoid the curse it carried with it. And the title track of an excellent sound-track album was their eighth consecutive UK chart-topper when released as a single.

Pop sound-tracks had never been known as good value buys, but the Beatles changed all that, just as they had revolutionized the pop album. Hitherto a couple of hit singles and a bunch of inferior filler tracks, the traditional album had been turned into an art form by the Fab Four. As Lennon and McCartney found their songwriting feet, the earlier smattering of cover versions had been squeezed out until each release was packed with only original material and potential hits. And if they weren't all hits for the Beatles themselves, alternative versions would often appear from nowhere: Joe Cocker, Marmalade and many other acts were to make a name for themselves by covering Beatles album tracks.

With Princess Margaret and Lord Snowdon attending the London premiere of *Help!* in July 1965, it was clear that moving into the world of cinema had put the Beatles even more firmly in the public eye. And Lennon, for one, was by now feeling the pressure. 'When *Help*! came out I was actually crying out for help. Most people think it's just a rock 'n' roll song...I'm singing about when I was so much younger, looking back at how easy it was.' Looking back to those eventful times in 1980 not long before his own death, Lennon likened himself to Elvis – and although he wasn't fat and drug-addicted like the King himself, he could quite easily have felt as cut off from reality.

A lot had happened in just three years; so much, in fact, that any film reflecting those real-life happenings would doubtless be considered too far-fetched to be feasible.

*A Hard Day's Night* had been the Beatles' first film, made on a low budget and a box-office smash in 1964. The title track was a million-seller, and the sound-track album proved equally successful. The plot certainly didn't stretch the four, portraying as it did the events of one day of a pop tour, yet Alun Owen's clever script gave each Beatle his own chance to shine.

It was in films that Lennon saw his future. 'I want no more success from being a record star,' he confessed. 'I'd like to see the Beatles making better and better films.'

The Beatles were, in fact, to make three more movies in addition to the aforementioned *Help!*, each one of them very different from the others. These were the animated *Yellow Submarine;* the final, fragmented documentary, *Let It Be;* and the made-for-television *Magical Mystery Tour;* which had a very

slight plot and was very critically reviewed, their first post-Epsteinmovie and a blot on an otherwise perfect artistic copybook.

Just sixty minutes in length, 1967's *Magical Mystery Tour* had stemmed from the McCartney song of the same name originally written for *Sgt Pepper,* and grew into a film of the Beatles and their friends touring the country in a bus. Even though the amount of original material amounted only to a double EP (later expanded to album length with additional tracks), the standout was Lennon's 'I Am The Walrus', its threatening lyric apparently typed line by line on a typewriter as the mood took him. With the Beatles, it seemed, even the occasional cloud had a silver lining.

Lennon's involvement in the 1967 Second World War movie *How I Won The War* (*below*) inevitably led to 'Beatles to split' headlines, but this was not going to happen just yet. Dick Lester, who had directed *A Hard Day's Night* and *Help!,* offered John the chance to take a break from the tour treadmill just days after the group returned to England from a US tour.

With the group's future as a live group in doubt, Lennon regarded his six-week sojourn as Private Gripweed as an experimental move. 'I didn't know

what to do,' Lennon later admitted. 'What do you do when you don't tour? Because there's no life. I spent six weeks thinking about what would I do when it stopped.' Paul, meanwhile, was thinking similarly and was composing the sound-track for (but not appearing in) *The Family Way.*

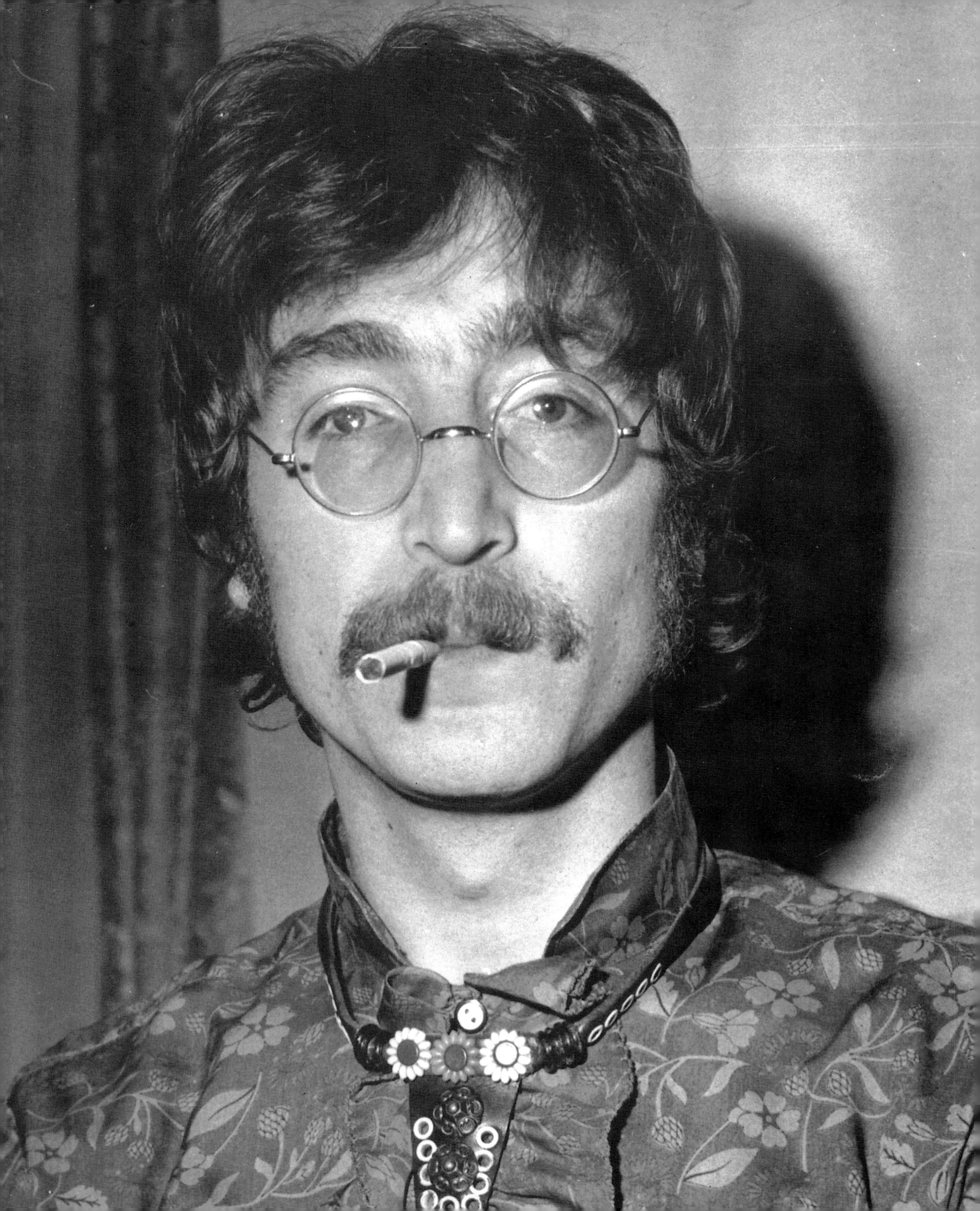

# Studio Psychedelia

POP MUSIC STARTED to take itself seriously with *Sgt Pepper,* released in 1967 and often quoted as the first ever 'rock' album. This was the album that made singles *passé* and buried forever the Beatles' hated Moptop image. It was to prove the yardstick against which all other albums were judged, and twenty years after its release it re-entered the British charts on its reissue in compact disc.

The album couldn't have been made without the influence of mind-expanding drugs. In Lennon's 'Lucy in the Sky with Diamonds', the initial letters spell out the song's true subject, although John insisted a painting by son Julian was the inspiration. But most of *Pepper* worked on a number of levels.

Press reaction to *Pepper* was ecstatic – and Lennon agreed. 'I keep saying I always preferred the double (White) album because my music is better…but *Pepper* was a peak all right.'

John and Paul usually took lead vocals on the songs they wrote themselves, the Lennon–McCartney credit being mainly for convenience. But 'A Day In The Life' showed that they could still collaborate when the mood took them. 'I'd written the first section' Lennon later explained, 'and let Paul hear it. He said what about this...a song he'd written on his own with no idea of what I was working on.' Having got the middle section, they needed 'a connecting bit, a growing noise to lead into the first bit,' said Lennon of the exciting climax of strings. 'Like all our songs,' he concluded, 'they

never became entities until the very end. They are developed all the time as we go along.'

Although the hopelessly sentimental songs were usually his partner's, Lennon turned to nostalgia to create 'Being For The Benefit Of Mr Kite'. The lyrics, he admitted, 'came from this old poster I'd bought at an antique shop advertising a variety show. There was no real work. I hardly made up a word, just connecting the lists together...'

Perhaps wisely, the Beatles' next project was something completely different – and even in the later days of glossy promotional videos it has never been equalled. Entitled *Our World,* this simultaneous broadcast effectively showcased their latest single, 'All You Need Is Love', to 400 million people in twenty-four countries in the first worldwide TV satellite link. It was also followed by something infinitely less celebratory: the death of manager and mentor Brian Epstein, only 32, after an overdose of sleeping pills.

The Beatles had become considerably less reliant on Epstein as their music and circle of acquaintances had developed; indeed, Paul had suggested that the Rolling Stones' Allen Klein should become their manager's business adviser. The Beatles may have outgrown their manager, but there was still a real sense of loss, and Lennon pinpointed Epstein's death as 'the disintegration...we broke up then.'

If drugs had played an ever-increasing role in the Beatles' music over the last three albums, then their flirtation with Eastern religion via the Maharishi Mahesh Yogi (*right*) could have been an attempt to turn the clock back and take a renewed grip on reality. John later condemned his drug activities, describing them as 'a game that everybody went through and I destroyed myself...'

Their interest in the East initially stemmed from Pattie Harrison's suggestion that they attend a lecture at London's Hilton Hotel. Significantly, perhaps, George was the only Beatle to pursue and retain an Eastern faith. The others followed him to Wales to meditate, but that was ruined by Epstein's death. In early 1968 the Beatles gave togetherness another try and jetted out to the Maharishi's ashram at Rishikesh, but Ringo stayed only ten days. Paul lasted nine weeks, John and George little longer.

John would later lampoon the Maharishi in 'Sexy Sadie', but he recognized the need to rebuild his life after too many LSD trips and too much drug experimentation. 'I was slowly putting myself together round about Maharishi time. Bit by bit, over a two-year period, I had destroyed my ego.'

Years later, Mick Jagger paid tribute to this, side of John Lennon. 'He did seem to be looking for something spiritual,' acknowledged the Rolling Stone.

Music, Love and Flowers
MONTEREY INTERNATIONAL POP FESTIVAL
SAFE AS MILK
SAFE AS MILK
international times

*Sgt Pepper* had promised to be the first step in an exciting if potentially dangerous musical journey. But having opened the doors of psychedelia, the Beatles seemed happy to let others continue the hazardous adventure. Their next album was to be quite different, its straightforward nature being apparent in both its title and plain cover.

*The Beatles,* otherwise known as the *White Album,* was a double LP with pictures of the individual Beatles included. This was symbolic, since most of the tracks were individual efforts: certainly the Lennon–McCartney songwriting partnership was now past history. That's not to say there weren't some great tracks on the album. The hard edge of 'Helter Skelter' and 'Revolution 1', the latter inspired by a demonstration outside the American Embassy in London and his first openly political song, were classic Lennon, while the more gentle 'Julia' was clearly about his mother. The writing was on the wall for the group whose whole had been so much more than the sum of the individuals who made it.

LOVE
L'AMOUR
IHR
LO
IS
C'EST
BRAUCH
QUE

ALS
ES
NEED
VOUS
LIEBE
AMOR

Premiered in July 1968 in the presence of all the Beatles except Ringo and released in January the following year, *Yellow Submarine* (*left*) was a well-loved animated adventure that sired an album of songs and a flood of spin-off merchandise that proved the public were far from tired of the Beatles.

But perhaps the Beatles were tired. Their final public appearance was played to the cameras, a group of Apple employees and bystanders from the roof of the Apple building in London on 20 January 1969. Originally, it had been intended to film both rehearsals and performance of a concert to an invited audience of 1500 at the Twickenham film studios, but a mixture of antipathy and apathy (acknowledged in the film and album's eventual title, *Let It Be*) killed it.

They'd long since finished performing for paying customers, of course – their last concert had been back in August 1966 at San Francisco's Candlestick Park. As the police moved in to stop the show, John left the stage with the wry parting comment, 'I hope we passed the audition.'

# The Ballad of Yoko

FROM MAY 1968, Lennon and McCartney took a back seat to a new partnership: John and Yoko. They first met at the Indica Gallery, where Yoko's exhibit of a blank canvas and a jar of nails fascinated John; their affair started soon afterwards. It was to be both a personal and professional relationship, as a series of *avant garde* albums like *Two Virgins* (1968), *Life With The Lions* and *Wedding Album* (both 1969) quickly proved.

Brian Epstein's death had left the band without a leader, and John wanted Allen Klein to take the helm. George and Ringo agreed, but Paul now nominated future brother-in-law John Eastman. Both group and management divided into two camps; there was to be no way back.

Shortly after the divorce from Cynthia came through, John and Yoko wed in Gibraltar on 20 March 1969, an event immortalized in 'The Ballad Of John and Yoko', the Beatles' last UK chart-topper.

John and Yoko spent their honeymoon in bed at the Amsterdam Hilton (*right*), turning the event into a very public peace stunt, the first of many. 'Why do you think we did so many things in bed?' asked Yoko. 'That was where we wanted to be. It was a strong physical reaction that lasted throughout our relationship.'

The anthemic 'Give Peace A Chance' was taped at one such 'Bed-in' and released in 1969 under the name Plastic Ono Band to become John's first hit record without the Beatles. 'I've always been politically minded and against the status quo,' he commented. 'It's just a basic working class thing.'

While *Get Back*, retitled and revamped as *Let It Be,* would be the last Beatles album on its appearance in 1970, *Abbey Road,* released late the previous year, was the final recording. Like *Get Back,* it was an attempt to return to the happy days of togetherness. It even included a jolly song for Ringo, just like old times, in 'Octopus's Garden'. A week before release, John announced his departure, though the decision wasn't immediately made public. 'We were discussing something in the office with Paul...and I kept saying "No, no, no" to everything he said. So it came to the point where I had to say something... "The group is over, I'm leaving."'

John had always liked his rock 'n' roll rough and ready, and with the Beatles falling apart around his ears, an ideal opportunity presented itself to return to live performance. The imaginary Plastic Ono Band invented for 'Give Peace A Chance' suddenly became flesh in the form of Eric Clapton, bassist Klaus Voorman (an old Hamburg friend) and drummer Alan White.

Their performance at the 1969 Toronto Peace Festival was taped for release as *Live Peace In Toronto,* and included a smattering of the rock 'n' roll greats John had been brought up on plus an early version of the future single 'Cold Turkey', complete with non-vocals from Yoko.

If such a consummate musician as Eric Clapton, available after the split of his super-group Cream, had any qualms about sharing a stage with Mrs Lennon, he chose not to make them public. The band also played the Lyceum in London in December, with George Harrison and Keith Moon of the Who also on stage in the 'Plastic Ono Super-group'. It was raw, spontaneous and as far from the Beatles as John had ever gone. A new decade beckoned, and the Fab Four seemed unlikely to figure in his plans.

In 1965 John had proclaimed he didn't want to be singing 'A Hard Day's Night' when he was 30. 'It would,' he said, 'be embarrassing.' This wish, made at the height of Beatlemania, was fulfilled with the 1970 release of *John Lennon/Plastic Ono Band,* his first solo album. Paul McCartney had already consigned the Beatles to history with the release of his first solo effort just two weeks before *Let It Be.* Yet listening to *Plastic Ono Band,* it was as if the Beatles had never existed. In 'God' John claimed, 'the dream is over…I was the Walrus but now I'm John', while 'Working Class Hero' totally rejected the same British society that had taken the Beatles to its collective heart.

There followed a series of singles that, as if to cock a snook at the album culture the Beatles had helped create, were to be unavailable on album for five years. 'Cold Turkey' was inspired by Janov's Primal Scream theory, and was a song Paul had not wanted the Beatles to record. 'Power To The People' was instantly and obviously political ('I think that everyone

should own everything equally'); the Phil Spector-produced 'Instant Karma' was more peacefully philosophical. Most successful of them all was 1972's 'Happy Xmas (War Is Over)', which became one of the classic seasonal singles, sneaking its message on to the radio in a wash of melody.

John (who had changed his middle name from Winston to Ono) had settled in New York's Greenwich Village, where he and Yoko felt more at home among the bohemian inhabitants. John's

English mansion at Tittenhurst near Reading had been cold and isolated, and the couple were happy to be back in the centre of things. Moreover, the British public's reaction to Yoko – who they regarded as 'the woman who broke up the Beatles' – had not been especially encouraging.

Lennon himself relished the prospect of life in the Big Apple. 'I like to live in the land of the free, and also if it's up to John Doe on the street, he either doesn't care about it or would be glad to have an old Beatle living here. I like to be here,' he added, 'because this is where the music came from, this is what influenced my whole life and got me where I am today.'

Once their bags were unpacked, John and Yoko seemed involved in almost every cause imaginable, from Irish republicanism to the campaigns to free black activists Angela Davis and John Sinclair. And this activity, not unnaturally, brought the pair to the attention of the FBI.

In March 1972 Lennon began a long-running fight to stay in the States when a visa extension granted just five days earlier was cancelled by the New York Office of Immigration. The reason given was a conviction for possessing soft drugs in 1968 (*above and right*), but a January concert at the Alice Tully Hall given without work permits seemed to have attracted more recent attention. They had performed from their seats, Yoko conducting the band with an apple. It seemed the pair might apply for US citizenship in a bid to beat the ban.

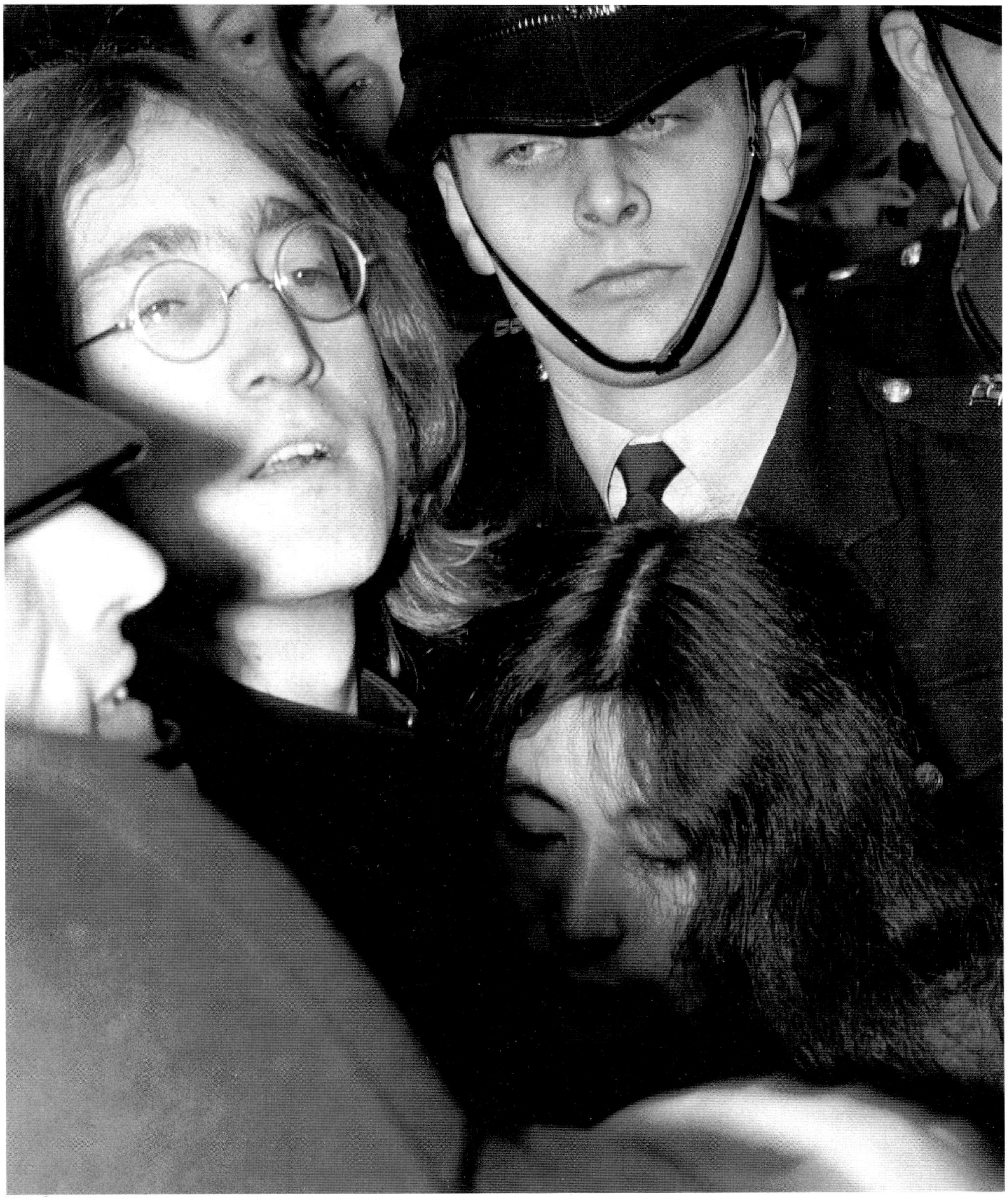

Three years later, the battle was won, but looking back on the affair John acknowledged it had affected his musical creativity, not to mention the intervening turmoil in his private life. 'It was getting to be a bug because I had to keep going to court and court cases got to be a way of life. I guess it showed in my work. Whatever happens to you happens in your work.'

# Double Fantasies

IF A SINGLE SONG were to encapsulate the public's perception of John Lennon the solo artist, then the title track of his 1971 album *Imagine* would be it. 'The lyric and the concept came from Yoko,' he later admitted, 'but those days I was a bit more selfish.' In contrast to that song's serene philosophy, the same album's 'How Do You Sleep?' revealed that bitterness against Paul McCartney remained.

American band Elephant's Memory backed John and Yoko on 1972's 'Some Time In New York City', which Lennon later disowned as 'journalism and not poetry. I was making an effort to reflect what was going on but pop music doesn't work like that.' John's post-Beatle career was proving fascinating in its unpredictability.

It's not
PRIZE

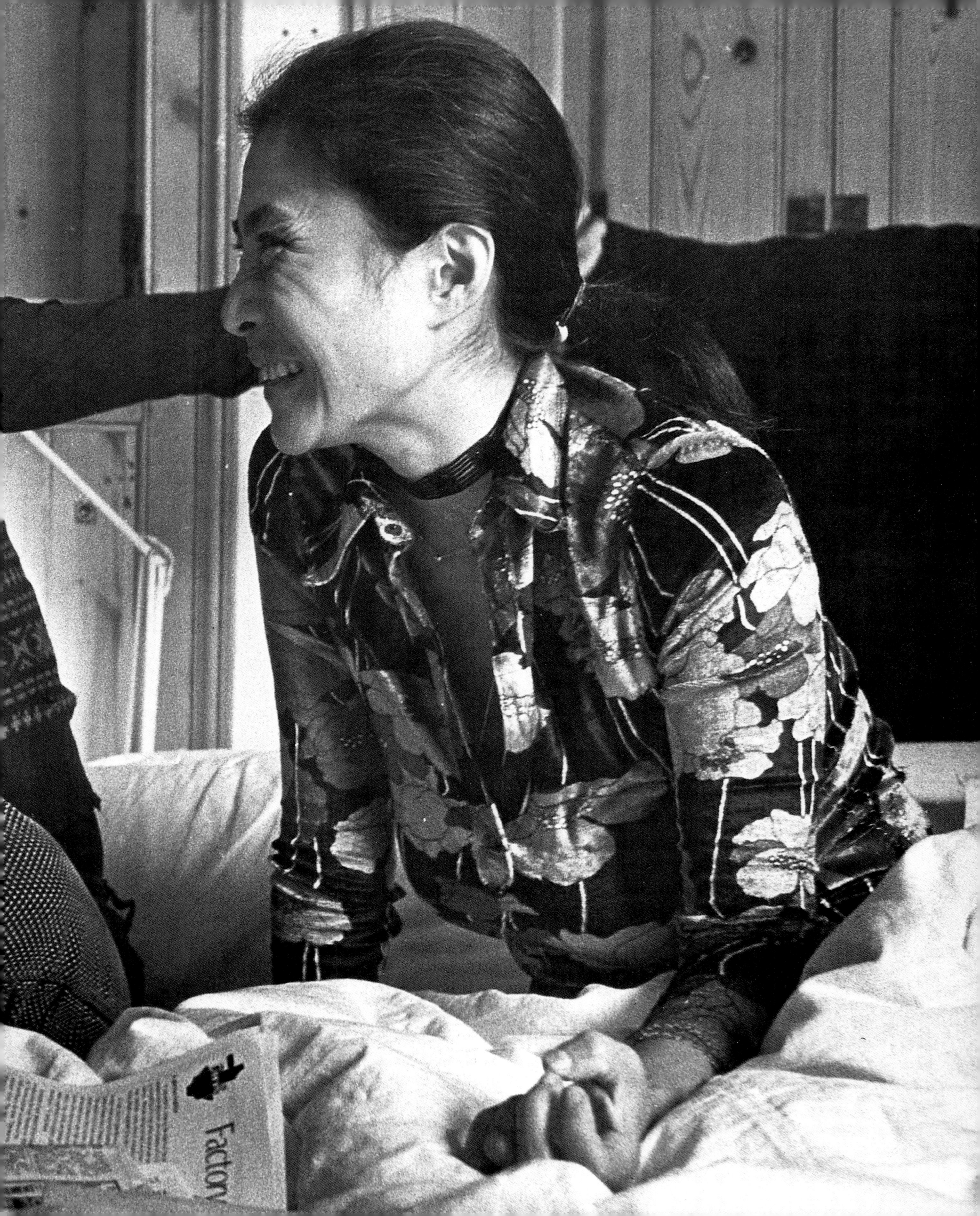
Factory

Life in New York (*above*) had not proved a bed of roses, and by the time 1973's *Mind Games* was released Lennon had split with Yoko and was dating her personal assistant, May Pang. Without Yoko at the helm, John steered a highly erratic course in the company of Harry Nilsson and volatile Who drummer Keith Moon. It was almost a return to the drunken camaraderie of the Hamburg days, with one exception: the full glare of the media spotlight, which highlighted every night-club ejection and unsavoury incident with relish, was always there.

STOP
Real Draft

Apple Tailori
by
Crittle

Fortunately, help was at hand in the person of Elton John. When 'Whatever Gets You Thru the Night', a single from the 1974 *Walls And Bridges* album, got to the top of the American chart, Lennon fulfilled a rash bet to sing it live, joining Elton on stage at New York's Madison Square Garden for what was to be his final live performance. The ecstatic crowd saw him sing his hit, plus 'Lucy in the Sky with Diamonds' and 'I Saw Her Standing There'.

If events on stage were somewhat unexpected, events backstage were equally newsworthy. John and Yoko met, made their peace and confirmed the reunion the following February, when they announced 'We need each other and have made the decision to try again.'

Domestic harmony was restored and Lennon was quite clearly content. 'I just sort of came home,' he later explained, adding flippantly 'I went out to get a newspaper or coffee somewhere and it took a year!' His 'lost weekend' was over. Ensconced in the Dakota, a gothic multi-storey building opposite Central Park that was home to many celebrated New Yorkers, he planned an entirely new career devoting his time to a most important new release: his son Sean, born on 9 October 1975.

Back in the dim and distant Sixties, Julian's upbringing had all too often been carried out in his father's absence, and John was not prepared to miss out again. An album of Fifties' cover versions, *Rock 'n' Roll,* and a compilation of original singles, *Shaved Fish,* were both released in 1975; neither broke new ground in musical terms, but the curiously titled *Shaved Fish* bore the equally strange legend 'A conspiracy of silence speaks louder than words'. Bar a single newspaper advertisement, this was to be the last the world would hear from Lennon for the next five years.

Yoko later explained his new-found philosophy in greater detail. 'John wanted to make a family and devote a lot of time to being with them. But, in spite of what people think, he didn't lock himself away. He wanted to concentrate on family rather than work and that meant being at home. But he used to go out. He'd go on long walks with Sean round New York or in Central Park. That was one of the things he cherished most, being normal.'

As months turned into years, John did most of the things any father would do with his wife and child, down to visiting the circus, where he'd queue for tickets like an ordinary Joe. He didn't wear any disguise, since that, as Yoko said, 'was not being normal. It simply shows how much a prisoner you are of your success.' It seemed John had loosened the chains of fame in a most extraordinary way.

Not that he ruled out further musical activities entirely. 'Yoko and I have decided to be with Sean as much as we can until we feel we can take time off...maybe when Sean is about three or four.'

A comeback, then, could be anticipated some time around 1978 or '79, but with new wave sweeping the music scene and groups like the Sex Pistols and the Clash noisily disowning rock's established idols, no one was holding their breath. 'I hate the thought of being famous for ever,' Lennon had once mused at the height of the Beatles' fame. 'What if we disappeared for years and years. Wouldn't that work?' The answer was clearly in the negative.

A prime mover in Lennon's return to music was David Geffen, the man who discovered the Eagles and Linda Ronstadt and, when boss of the Asylum label, played a major role in creating the genre we now know as West Coast or 'soft' rock. Now with a new, self-named label, he knew that masterminding John's artistic renaissance would put Geffen Records well and truly on the map. And as time went by he got his wish.

The couple inked a contract with Geffen on the eve of Lennon's fortieth birthday, spending the autumn holed up in New York's Record Plant recording an album that would be named after an orchid John had spotted while on a recreational trip to Bermuda.

Five years of waiting came to an end with the November 1980 release of *Double Fantasy,* an album credited to John and Yoko jointly and acclaimed as his best work since *Plastic Ono Band.* Its simplicity reflected an earlier, less troubled period of Lennon's life, the lyrics of songs like 'Watching The Wheels' reflecting his new philosophy of life and love for his son.

Understandably, the Lennons' renaissance gathered many acres of press coverage. *Newsweek* did a special interview, *Playboy* asked them to be the main interview of their Christmas 1980 issue, while *Esquire* did a cover story. The single '(Just Like) Starting Over' entered the US Top Forty in late November to become John's first record since 'Stand By Me' five and a half long years earlier.

Unknown to John and Yoko, this publicity was to inspire the attention not only of well-meaning fans but also of one man in particular, whose feelings towards the ex-Beatle were far from affectionate.

John had rediscovered his urge to make music, and there seemed no limit to what the world could

LIVES ON

expect in the coming decade. Then on 8 December 1980 just before 11 p.m. Mark Chapman pulled a Smith & Wesson .38 revolver and ended John's life with five bullets to the upper body.

With supreme irony, the feature of New York life John had cherished most was the ability to walk around unrecognized and unbothered. 'It took me two years to unwind,' he had admitted. 'I would be walking round tense like that waiting for someone to say something or jump on me... I can go right out and go into a restaurant or go to the movies. You know how great that is?'

On the fateful night of 8 December Lennon and Yoko had been returning from the studio, where they had been working on Yoko's forthcoming single, 'Walking On Thin Ice'. Chapman, for whom Lennon had ironically signed an album sleeve only hours before, was an unknown 25-year-old security guard from Hawaii, obsessed with the idea that he was Lennon. The world, it seemed, was not big enough for the two of them...

At first, Yoko didn't realize John had been hit. As he fell to his knees, he cried 'I'm shot!'; only then did the terrible truth dawn. The Dakota doorman covered him with his coat, but John was already only semi-conscious. He was rushed to the Roosevelt Memorial Hospital, but was pronounced dead half an hour after arrival.

Mark Chapman, meanwhile, was still outside the building calmly reading from J.D. Salinger's classic novel *Catcher in the Rye*. He had dropped the gun by then, and for all the world looked like an innocent bystander. 'Do you know what you just did?' blurted the now-coatless doorman. 'I just shot John Lennon,' Chapman quietly responded.

EXTRA
NEW YORK POST
JOHN LENNON SHOT DEA
Gunned down at point-bla
His wife Yoko watches
HUNTING
POL

As with John F. Kennedy's assassination and the first moon landing, everyone can remember where they were when they heard the news: John Lennon is dead. Crowds gathered outside the Dakota and in Liverpool, as notables from President Reagan downwards rushed to express their shock, anger and sympathy. John's fellow Beatles were cautious in their public reaction, especially when Paul's immediate off-guard comment, 'It's a drag', was widely reported in a way intended to underline supposed feelings of enmity.

Yoko herself, still in shock, read the following simple statement: 'John loved and prayed for the human race. Please do the same for him.' She later requested a ten-minute silent vigil, which was held on 14 December, and in which millions of fans worldwide participated, ironically showing in silence their respect for a master of popular music.

When Beatlemania ruled, it wasn't unusual to see two, three or more of the group's singles in the charts simultaneously, but this was different. The record business had been waiting for years for the new Beatles, and ironically it was the killing of an old one that made Christmas 1980 an even more profitable period than usual. '(Just Like) Starting Over', 'Imagine' and 'Woman' gave John Lennon three British Number One singles in just seven weeks.

In 1982 *The John Lennon Collection* combined the cream of his post-Beatles period with the pick of *Double Fantasy,* and topped the chart on the first anniversary of his death. And in 1990, the tenth anniversary of his death and the fiftieth anniversary of his birth, his home city of Liverpool played host to a celebration of his life and memory with Yoko, Sean, Joe Cocker, Lou Reed and a host of artists he'd inspired.

So what would John Lennon have been creating in the Eighties and Nineties? It seems unlikely that he'd voluntarily have stepped back on to the record treadmill he'd grown to hate so much, yet given the amount of previously unreleased material that appeared after *Double Fantasy,* it's likely he'd have gone on releasing albums through the Eighties.

He'd also no doubt have played at least an advisory role in the career of his son Julian. After a two-million-selling debut LP, *Valotte,* released in 1984,

Julian's career took a commercial nose-dive, only to resurface in 1991 with a 'Strawberry Fields' soundalike single, 'Saltwater'. Given John's 'active parenthood' stance towards Sean, he'd undoubtedly have passed on the benefit of his experience to his elder son and possibly helped iron out the peaks and troughs of his career.

One thing John would have had to bear were the incessant demands for a Beatles reunion, a topic only his death seemed able to banish from the pop papers.

Just weeks before his own death, Lennon had registered his disapproval of the hero-worship of dead teen idols like Fifties' film star James Dean and

Seventies' punk-rocker Sid Vicious. It was a point Paul McCartney restated in 1990. 'If John was alive now,' he commented, 'he'd be the first to laugh at all this. If all this fuss had been made over someone else, he would have been cracking up by now.'

Whatever his former songwriting colleague's reservations, there is no doubt that the John Lennon legend lives on: an immortal who emerged from the notably ephemeral pop music world.

# Acknowledgements

*Managing Editor:* Lesley McOwan
*Design:* Robert Mathias
*Production:* Nick Thompson
*Picture Research:* Emily Hedges
*Editor:* Barbara Horn

The Publishers should like to thank the following organizations for their kind permission to reproduce the photographs in this book:-

Aquarius Picture Library; 10-11, 23 top, 26-27, 29; The Bettmann Archive; 58-9; Camera Press; 13, 54, 81, /Tom Blau; 64, 66 /Tom Hanley; 78-79, /Ben Ross; 83, 90; Ronald Grant Archive/Apple Corporation Ltd.; 73 right; Hulton Picture Company; 20, 35, 39 top, 55, 59 top right, 63, 67, 70-71, 75, 76; The Kobal Collection; 48, 49, 72-3; London Features International; 6, 34, 37, 40-41, 80, 91; Popperfoto; 31, 32-33, 36, 39 bottom, 42, 50, 68, 69, 74, 94; Rex Features; 8, 9, 14-15, 17, 21, 24, 28, 30, 43, 44, 46-47, 56-57, 82, /Nick Elgar; 96, /Hatami; 18-19, 22-23, /Sipa; 95; Springer/Bettmann Film Archive; 3, 5, 51; Topham Picture Source; 12, 16, 60-61, 62; UPI/Bettmann; 52, 84-85, 86-87, 89, 92-3.